MEMORY MIRACLES

Boosting Recall Skills for Kids and Teens

CHRIS LEO

MEMORY MIRACLES

By Rev. Chris Leo

First Published February 2024

© Palace Media

All Rights Reserved

No part of this work may be reproduced or transmitted in any form or by any means without the express permission of the author and/or the publishers

CONTENTS

INTRODUCTION 7

WHY I WROTE THIS BOOK 10

CHAPTER 1 15
THE POWER OF FAITH AND MEMORY 15

Faith as a Foundation 16
Biblical Examples of Memory 16
The Role of Trust and Belief 17
The Meeting Point of Faith and Learning .. 18
Faith as a Source of Hope 18
The Miraculous Potential of Faith 19

CHAPTER 2 21
BIBLICAL MEMORY TECHNIQUES 21

Memorizing Scripture: The Heart of Faith . 22
Storytelling and Parables: An Ancient Tradition 22
Repetition and Recitation 23
Song and Praise: A Melodic Reminder 24
Visual Aids and Symbolism: A Visual Journey 25
Group Study and Memorization: Strength in Community 25

CHAPTER 3 27
PRAYERS FOR MEMORY MASTERY .. 27
The Prayer of Solomon: Seeking Wisdom and Understanding 28
The Prayer of Jabez: Seeking Blessings and Enlarged Territory 28
The Prayer of Hannah: Gratitude and Surrender 29
The Prayer of Faith: Believing in God's Promises 30
Affirmations of Strength and Confidence ... 30
Gratitude and Praise: A Heart of Thanksgiving 31

CHAPTER 4 33
SCRIPTURE MEMORIZATION STRATEGIES 33
Verse Chunking Technique 34
Repetition and Review 35
Picturing and Imagery 36
Association with Personal Experiences 36
Set Scripture to Music 37
Prayer and Meditation 37
Application in Daily Life 38
Group Memorization and Accountability ...38
Celebrate Milestones and Progress 39
Perseverance and Patience 39

CHAPTER 5 41
THE MEMORY MIRACLE OF MIRACLES
.... 41
The Miracle of Feeding the Multitudes 42
The Healing of the Blind and Deaf 43
The Resurrection of Lazarus 43
The Healing of the Paralyzed Man 44
The Miracle of Pentecost 44
The Legacy of Saints and Martyrs 45
The Miracle of Conversion and Transformation 46
The Memory Miracle of Salvation 46

CHAPTER 6 49
BUILDING A MEMORY FOUNDATION WITH FAITH 49
Faith as the Cornerstone of Memory 50
Daily Devotions and Scripture Study 50
Prayer and Meditation Practices 51
Journaling and Reflection 52
Memorization and Application 53
Community and Fellowship 54
Faithful Persistence and Perseverance 55

CHAPTER 7 57
OVERCOMING MEMORY CHALLENGES THROUGH FAITH 57
Acknowledging Memory Challenges 58

Turning to God in Prayer 58
Trusting in God's Provision 59
Seeking Strength in Scripture 60
Practicing Patience and Perseverance 60
Embracing a Growth Mindset 61
Drawing Strength from Community 62
Celebrating Progress and Growth 63

CHAPTER 8 65
MEMORY MIRACLES IN EVERYDAY LIFE 65
Remembering God's Promises 66
Recalling Lessons Learned 66
Retaining Knowledge and Skills 67
Recounting Acts of Kindness and Gratitude 68
Revisiting Sacred Traditions and Rituals 69
Reflecting on Miracles and Testimonies 70
Rejoicing in the Miracle of Salvation 71

CHAPTER 9 73
THE ROLE OF COMMUNITY AND FELLOWSHIP 73
Supportive Community Bonds 74
Encouragement and Accountability 75
Shared Learning and Growth 76
Prayer and Intercession 77
Celebrating Milestones and Achievements . 78

Cultivating Compassion and Empathy 79
Embracing Diversity and Inclusion 79

CHAPTER 10 81
EMBRACING GROWTH MINDSET IN MEMORY MASTERY 81
Understanding Growth Mindset 82
Embracing Challenges 82
Learning from Mistakes 83
Seeking Feedback and Guidance 84
Cultivating Perseverance and Resilience 85
Celebrating Progress and Success 85

CONCLUSION 89
Caution 89

INTRODUCTION

The world we live in is a on a fast lane in almost every area. It has become a world where information bombardment is constant and distractions are abundant. This is seriously affecting the minds of the average person including young people. Therefore, having a strong memory is more crucial than ever. For children and teenagers navigating through school, extracurricular activities, and the challenges of growing up, to develop effective memory skills can be a game-changer.

In this book, we embark on a journey to unlock the secrets of memory mastery specifically tailored for young learners. From mnemonics to visualization techniques, from mind mapping to the power of association, we explore a myriad of strategies designed to enhance memory retention, comprehension, and recall. Nevertheless, more than just memorizing facts or figures, this book is about empowering young minds to become active participants in their own learning journey.

Throughout these pages, children and teens will discover not only how to remember information more effectively but also how to engage with learning in a meaningful and enjoyable way. Memory is not just about rote memorization; it is about understanding, connecting, and applying knowledge in various contexts. It is about building a foundation of learning that lasts a lifetime.

As we plunge into the fascinating world of memory miracles, let us embark with open minds, curious hearts, and a spirit of adventure. Together, we will uncover the wonders of the human mind and unleash the full potential of our memory capabilities. So, get ready to embark on an unforgettable journey of discovery, empowerment, and memory miracles. Now, the adventure begins!

WHY I WROTE THIS BOOK

With a passion for seeing people do better in life, and a strong appeal for advanced and updated knowledge, I have the pleasure of writing books as this to actualize them. These same reasons moved me to pen *Memory Miracles*. Besides, witnessing the struggles many teens face due to memory loss ignited a sense of urgency within me to address this global trend head-on.

In our world today, where information overload is the norm, the stakes for memory mastery have never been higher. Teens and young adults struggling with memory challenges not only face academic hurdles but also encounter obstacles in everyday life. From forgetting important details to feeling overwhelmed in school and social settings, the impact of memory loss can be profound.

As a parent, I have witnessed the heartache and frustration experienced by families navigating the complexities of memory-related issues. The emotional toll and practical challenges parents endure while supporting their teens through memory difficulties are undeniable.

However, amidst these challenges lies a glimmer of hope and possibility. I envision a world filled with young people equipped with the brainpower to thrive in every aspect of their lives. Through *Memory Miracles*, I aim to empower teens, parents, and educators with practical strategies and insights to unlock the full potential of their memory capabilities.

My fervent desire is to see young minds emboldened by the tools and techniques shared in this book, enabling them to conquer academic challenges, navigate social interactions with confidence, and ultimately, lead fulfilling lives fueled by the power of memory mastery.

Join me on this positively impacting journey as we pave the way for a future where memory miracles abound, and young people everywhere unlock the full potential of their brilliant minds. Let us build a world where memory is not a limitation but a source of boundless opportunity and empowerment.

Rev. Chris Leo

CHAPTER 1

THE POWER OF FAITH AND MEMORY

> Introducing the idea that faith can play a role in memory enhancement. Explore stories from the Bible where faith and memory intersect, demonstrating how belief and trust can boost recall skills.

Welcome, young believers, to the first chapter of this book. In this chapter, we embark on a journey to explore the extraordinary connection between faith and memory, discovering how the two link to create miracles of ability to remember.

Of course, expect some examples of this in the Bible and the positive result that followed each example. Let us now move into the pages of the faith and memory.

Faith as a Foundation

Faith is more than just belief – a foundation upon which we build our lives. Just as a strong foundation supports a solid structure, faith provides the bedrock for our memory journey. With faith, we believe in the possibility of memory miracles, trusting in God's guidance and provision.

Biblical Examples of Memory

The Bible is rich with examples of individuals who relied on their memory to uphold their faith and share God's word. Moses recalled God's commandments to His people on Mount Sinai. He wrote them down for all the people to read and obey.

Jesus recited the scripture in the face of temptation, in the wilderness. He was able to defeat Satan and overcome. Many biblical figures demonstrated the power of memory as a tool for spiritual growth and resilience.

The Role of Trust and Belief

At the heart of faith is trust – trust in God's promises, trust in His guidance, and trust in His ability to work miracles in our lives. When we approach memory challenges with belief and trust, we open ourselves to the possibility of divine intervention and supernatural assistance.

The Meeting Point of Faith and Learning

Our faith journey is interwoven with our learning journey. As we study scripture and grow in knowledge of God's word, our memory skills are improved and strengthened. Through prayer and meditation, we invite God's presence into our memory practice, seeking His wisdom and illumination.

Faith as a Source of Hope

In times of struggle and difficulty, faith serves as a beacon of hope, illuminating the path forward. When faced with memory challenges, we turn to God in prayer, seeking His comfort and guidance. Through faith, we find strength and perseverance to overcome obstacles and pursue excellence in memory recall.

The Miraculous Potential of Faith

When we combine faith with our memory practice, we tap into a reservoir of miraculous potential. With God's help, we can achieve feats of memory that surpass our expectations and defy the limits of human understanding. Through faith, all things are possible—including memory miracles.

As we embark on this journey of faith and memory, let us open our hearts to

God's guiding hand and trust in His plan for our memory growth. With faith as our compass, we step forward into the realm of memory miracles, ready to witness the extraordinary work of God in our recall skills. Amen.

CHAPTER 2

BIBLICAL MEMORY TECHNIQUES

> Research into the memory techniques and practices found within the Bible itself. From memorizing verses to recounting stories, discover how biblical figures utilized memory to strengthen their faith and share God's word.

Welcome back, young believers, to the enriching journey. In this chapter, we dig into the timeless wisdom of the Bible to uncover powerful memory techniques and practices.

Memorizing Scripture: The Heart of Faith

Scripture memorization lies at the heart of our faith journey. In Psalm 119:11, David wrote,

"I have hidden your word in my heart that I might not sin against you."

This verse emphasizes the importance of internalizing God's word through memorization, allowing it to guide our thoughts, actions, and decisions.

Storytelling and Parables: An Ancient Tradition

Throughout the Bible, we encounter captivating stories and parables that convey profound truths. Jesus often used parables to teach his disciples and the crowds, illustrating spiritual principles through vivid narratives. By immersing ourselves in these stories and committing them to memory, we gain insight into God's character and purposes.

Repetition and Recitation

In Deuteronomy 6:6-7, we are instructed,

"These commandments that I give you today are to be on your hearts. Impress them on your children. Talk about them when you sit at home and when you walk along the road, when you lie down and when you get up."

This passage highlights the importance of repetition and recitation in embedding God's commandments in our hearts and minds.

Song and Praise: A Melodic Reminder

In Colossians 3:16, we are encouraged to *"let the message of Christ dwell among you richly as you teach and admonish one another with all wisdom through psalms, hymns, and songs from the Spirit, singing to God with gratitude in your hearts."*

Singing hymns and spiritual songs not only lifts our spirits but also reinforces key biblical truths in our memory through melody and rhythm.

Visual Aids and Symbolism: A Visual Journey

Throughout the Bible, we encounter rich symbolism and imagery that engage our senses and spark our imagination. From the rainbow as a symbol of God's covenant with Noah to the parable of the sower scattering seeds, visual aids and symbolism enhance our understanding and retention of biblical concepts.

Group Study and Memorization: Strength in Community

In Acts 2:42, we read,

"They devoted themselves to the apostles' teaching and to fellowship, to the breaking of bread and to prayer."

This verse underscores the importance of communal study and memorization, where believers come together to learn, share, and encourage one another in their faith journey.

As we explore these biblical memory techniques, let us draw inspiration from the wisdom of Scripture and the example of faithful men and women who have gone before us. May we commit ourselves to the diligent study and memorization of God's word, allowing it to transform our hearts, minds, and lives. Amen.

CHAPTER 3

PRAYERS FOR MEMORY MASTERY

> Introduce prayers and affirmations specifically tailored to help children and teens improve their memory. Explore the spiritual aspect of memory enhancement and the role of prayer in seeking divine guidance for recall skills.

Dear young believers, welcome once again. In this chapter, we look into the power of prayer as a good tool for memory mastery. Let us explore prayers and affirmations specifically tailored to help you strengthen your memory.

The Prayer of Solomon: Seeking Wisdom and Understanding

In 1 Kings 3:9, Solomon prayed to the Lord, saying, *"So give your servant a discerning heart to govern your people and to distinguish between right and wrong."*

Like Solomon, let us pray for wisdom and understanding in our pursuit of memory mastery, asking God to guide our minds and illuminate our paths.

The Prayer of Jabez: Seeking Blessings and Enlarged Territory

In 1 Chronicles 4:10, Jabez cried out to the God of Israel, saying, *"Oh, that you would bless me and enlarge my territory! Let your hand be with me, and keep me from harm so that I will be free from pain."*

Let us emulate Jabez's boldness in seeking God's blessings and favor as we embark on our memory journey, trusting in His provision and protection.

The Prayer of Hannah: Gratitude and Surrender

In 1 Samuel 2:1, Hannah prayed,

"My heart rejoices in the Lord; in the Lord my horn is lifted high. My mouth boasts over my enemies, for I delight in your deliverance."

Let us echo Hannah's spirit of gratitude and surrender, offering prayers of thanksgiving for the gift of memory and committing our minds to God's care and guidance.

The Prayer of Faith: Believing in God's Promises

In Mark 11:24, Jesus declared, ***"Therefore I tell you, whatever you ask for in prayer, believe that you have received it, and it will be yours."*** Let us approach our prayers for memory mastery with unwavering faith, trusting in God's promises and believing that He will grant us the wisdom, clarity, and retention we seek.

Affirmations of Strength and Confidence

In times of doubt and uncertainty, let us speak words of strength and confidence over our minds and memories. Repeat affirmations such as:

"I have a sharp and focused mind,"

"I remember with clarity and ease," and

"God's wisdom guides my memory."

Through positive affirmations, we reinforce our belief in God's ability to work miracles in our memory.

Gratitude and Praise: A Heart of Thanksgiving

Finally, let us cultivate a heart of gratitude and praise as we lift our prayers for memory mastery. In Philippians 4:6-7, we are reminded,

"Do not be anxious about anything, but in every situation, by prayer and petition, with thanksgiving, present your requests to God. And the peace of God, which transcends all understanding, will guard your hearts and your minds in Christ Jesus."

Dear friends, as we offer our prayers and affirmations for memory mastery, may we trust in God's faithfulness and provision. I pray our hearts be filled with gratitude and praise as we witness the miraculous work of God in our minds and memories. Amen.

CHAPTER 4

SCRIPTURE MEMORIZATION STRATEGIES

> Provide practical tips and techniques for memorizing Bible verses and passages. Incorporate fun games, activities, and mnemonic devices designed to engage young minds and strengthen their recall of scripture.

Hello, young disciples. In this chapter, we embark on an exciting journey to explore effective strategies for memorizing scripture – the living word of God.

To memorize scripture is important in the life of every Christian even children and youths. To memorize means to read out words and try to remember them without reading. Now, let us see some techniques or strategies for memorizing scriptural texts.

Verse Chunking Technique

Chunking means breaking down into smaller units for easy recall. Break down longer passages of scripture into smaller chunks or sections. Focus on memorizing one chunk at a time, gradually building upon each section until you can recite the entire passage with ease.

For example, break down Psalm 23 into manageable chunks: "The Lord is my shepherd; I shall not want."

Once you have memorized this first line, then, you can proceed to the next line: "He makes me to lie down in green pastures".

Commit this to memory and when you are sure you can recite it without looking at the text, then, go on to the next line until you memorize the entire chapter fully.

Repetition and Review

Repetition is key to memory retention. Repeat the verses you are memorizing regularly, preferably daily. Use flashcards, write the verses down, or recite them aloud. Avoid musing it in your heart when you are starting this exercise. Instead, say it aloud so you can hear yourself. Do not worry if someone else is listening to you. Regular review helps reinforce neural pathways in your brain, making the scripture verses stick.

Picturing and Imagery

Visualize the scenes and messages described in the scripture verses. Create vivid mental images that represent the meaning and context of the verses. For example, picture Jesus walking on water as you memorize the passage from Matthew 14:25-27.

Association with Personal Experiences

Relate the scripture verses to your own life experiences. Connect the messages of the verses to moments when you've felt God's presence, received His blessings, or faced challenges. Personal associations make the verses more meaningful and memorable.

Set Scripture to Music

Transform scripture verses into catchy tunes or songs. Set the words to familiar melodies or compose your own tunes. Singing scripture verses will add a melodic element that enhances memory retention and makes memorization enjoyable.

Prayer and Meditation

Before memorizing scripture, pray for God's guidance and understanding. Ask the Holy Spirit to illuminate the meaning of the verses and help you internalize them deeply. Spend time meditating on the verses, reflecting on their significance in your life.

Application in Daily Life

Apply the scripture verses you have memorized to real-life situations. Practice living out the principles and teachings found in the verses. Share them with others, discuss their relevance, and encourage one another in faith.

Group Memorization and Accountability

Join a scripture memorization group or partner with a friend to memorize verses together. Hold each other accountable and provide support and encouragement along the way. Memorizing scripture becomes a communal journey of faith and growth.

Celebrate Milestones and Progress

Celebrate each milestone and progress you make in scripture memorization. Recognize the effort and dedication you have put into memorizing God's word. Share your achievements with your family, friends, and church community.

Perseverance and Patience

Remember that scripture memorization is a journey that requires perseverance and patience. Be patient with yourself as you learn and grow. Trust in God's timing and His ability to equip you with the memory skills you need.

As you embark on the adventure of scripture memorization, the word of God dwells richly in your hearts and minds. I see you experience the joy and transformation that come from hiding His word in your heart. Amen.

CHAPTER 5

THE MEMORY MIRACLE OF MIRACLES

> Share inspiring stories of individuals who experienced miraculous improvements in memory through their faith and belief in God's power. These stories serve as examples of how divine intervention can lead to remarkable memory transformations.

Welcome, young believers. Now let us explore the miraculous potential of memory through the lens of faith, drawing inspiration from biblical accounts and historical references. These will facilitate the process of activating your mind for super performance as you remember these miracles and commit them to your memory always.

The Miracle of Feeding the Multitudes

In Matthew 14:13-21, we read about the miraculous feeding of the five thousand. Jesus took five loaves of bread and two fish, blessed them, and fed a multitude of people with abundance left over. Twelve baskets full! That was awesomely miraculous, right.

This miraculous event shows the power of divine provision and abundance – a memory miracle beyond human comprehension. You can always relate to it.

The Healing of the Blind and Deaf

In Mark 7:31-37, Jesus healed a deaf and mute man, restoring his hearing and speech. This miraculous encounter demonstrates the transformative power of memory in restoring wholeness and restoring lives. Through God's miraculous intervention, Jesus restored the man's memory of sound and speech miraculously.

The Resurrection of Lazarus

In John 11:1-44, Jesus raised Lazarus from the dead, calling him forth from the tomb after four days. This miraculous event illustrates the power of memory in overcoming death and bringing new life. Through Jesus' words and divine authority, Lazarus' memory was restored, and he emerged from the grave alive and whole.

The Healing of the Paralyzed Man

In Luke 5:17-26, Jesus healed a paralyzed man lowered through the roof by his friends. Before healing him, Jesus forgave the man's sins, demonstrating the inseparable connection between spiritual and physical healing. Through this miraculous encounter, the paralyzed man's memory of wholeness and restoration was miraculously restored.

The Miracle of Pentecost

In Acts 2:1-4, we read about the miraculous outpouring of the Holy

Spirit on the day of Pentecost. As the disciples gathered in the upper room, they were filled with the Holy Spirit and began speaking in other tongues. This miraculous event enabled the disciples to remember and proclaim the wonders of God's works to people from every nation and language.

The Legacy of Saints and Martyrs

Throughout history, countless saints and martyrs have demonstrated extraordinary memory miracles through their unwavering faith and devotion to God. From the memorization of scripture to the preservation of sacred traditions, their memory of God's truth and love has inspired generations of believers.

The Miracle of Conversion and Transformation

Countless individuals have experienced memory miracles through encounters with Jesus Christ and the power of the Holy Spirit. From hardened hearts transformed by grace to lives renewed by the truth of God's word, these stories of conversion and transformation testify to the miraculous work of memory in the lives of believers.

The Memory Miracle of Salvation

Ultimately, the greatest memory miracle of all is the gift of salvation through Jesus Christ. In Ephesians 2:8-9, we are reminded, *"For it is by grace you have been saved, through faith – and this is not from yourselves, it is the gift of God – not by works, so that no one can boast."* Through the power of Christ's sacrifice and resurrection, our memories are redeemed, and we are reconciled to God for eternity.

As we reflect on these memory miracles, may we be inspired to trust in God's power and provision in our own lives. May our memories be filled with the wonders of His love and the miracles of His grace. Amen.

CHAPTER 6

BUILDING A MEMORY FOUNDATION WITH FAITH

> Offer guidance on cultivating a strong memory foundation rooted in faith and spiritual practices. Explore the connection between spiritual discipline, prayer, and memory development in children and teens.

Welcome back, young disciples. In this chapter, we look into the importance of building a strong memory foundation rooted in faith and spiritual practices. Faith and works go hand in glove. There is no faith without works. Therefore, with faith, you can build a sound memory.

Faith as the Cornerstone of Memory

Just as a building requires a solid foundation to stand tall and strong, our memory skills rely on a foundation of faith to flourish. In Matthew 7:24-25, Jesus compares the wise builder who builds his house on a rock to the foolish builder who builds on sand. Let us be like the wise builder, establishing our memory foundation on the rock-solid truth of God's word.

Daily Devotions and Scripture Study

Set aside time each day for personal devotions and scripture study. Make it a habit to read and meditate on God's word, allowing His truth to penetrate your heart and mind. In Psalm 119:105, we are reminded, *"Your word is a lamp for my feet, a light on my path."* Let God's word illuminate your memory journey and guide you in the way of truth.

Prayer and Meditation Practices

Cultivate a lifestyle of prayer and meditation, inviting God's presence into every aspect of your life, including your memory practice.

In Philippians 4:6-7, we are encouraged, *"Do not be anxious about anything, but in every situation, by prayer and petition, with thanksgiving, present your requests to God. And the peace of God, which transcends all understanding, will guard your hearts and your minds in Christ Jesus."* Through prayer and meditation, we surrender our memory challenges to God and trust in His provision.

Journaling and Reflection

Keep a journal to record your thoughts, prayers, and reflections on scripture. Write down key verses, insights, and revelations that resonate with you. Reflect on how God's word applies to your life and how it can inform your memory practice.

In Habakkuk 2:2, we read, *"Write down the revelation and make it plain on tablets so that a herald may run with it."* Let your journal be a witness to God's faithfulness and a testament to His work in your memory journey.

Memorization and Application

Apply the principles and teachings of scripture to your memory practice. Choose verses that speak to your heart and align with your goals for memory improvement. Memorize them diligently and apply them to your daily life.

In James 1:22, we are urged, ***"Do not merely listen to the word, and so deceive yourselves. Do what it says."*** Let the words of scripture take root in your memory and bear fruit in your actions.

Community and Fellowship

Surround yourself with a community of believers who can support and encourage you in your memory journey. Join a small group, youth ministry, or Bible study where you can share insights, pray for one another, and hold each other accountable.

In Hebrews 10:24-25, we are exhorted, *"And let us consider how we may spur one another on toward love and good deeds, not giving up meeting together, as some are in the habit of doing, but encouraging one another—and all the more as you see the Day approaching."* Together, we can strengthen our memory foundations and grow in faith.

Faithful Persistence and Perseverance

Remember that building a memory foundation with faith requires faithful persistence and perseverance. There will be challenges and obstacles along the way, but with God's strength and guidance, you can overcome them.

In Galatians 6:9, we are reminded, ***"Let us not become weary in doing good, for at the proper time we will reap a harvest if we do not give up."*** Keep pressing forward in faith, trusting that God will honor your efforts and bless your memory journey.

As you build a memory foundation with faith, may you be rooted and established in God's love, grounded in

His truth, and strengthened by His Spirit. Allow your memory skills flourish as you walk in faith and obedience, bringing glory to God in all that you do. Amen.

CHAPTER 7

OVERCOMING MEMORY CHALLENGES THROUGH FAITH

> Address common memory challenges faced by children and teens, providing biblical wisdom and encouragement to overcome obstacles. Offer practical strategies and scriptures for navigating memory difficulties with faith and resilience.

Dear young believers. In this chapter, we confront the memory challenges that we face and discover how faith can be our guiding light in overcoming them.

Acknowledging Memory Challenges

It is important to recognize that everyone faces memory challenges at some point in their lives. Whether it is forgetting names, struggling to remember facts for a test, or experiencing difficulty recalling important information, we all encounter moments when our memory seems to falter.

Turning to God in Prayer

When faced with memory challenges, our first response should be to turn to God in prayer. In Philippians 4:6-7, we are encouraged, ***"Do not be anxious about anything, but in every situation, by prayer and petition, with thanksgiving,*** *present your requests to God. And the peace of God, which transcends all understanding, will guard your hearts and your minds in Christ Jesus."* Through prayer, we invite God's peace and guidance into our memory struggles.

Trusting in God's Provision

As we pray, we trust in God's provision and wisdom to help us overcome our memory challenges. In Proverbs 3:5-6, we are reminded, *"Trust in the Lord with all your heart and lean not on your own understanding; in all your ways submit to him, and he will make your paths straight."* By surrendering our memory struggles to God, we acknowledge His sovereignty and trust in His divine guidance.

Seeking Strength in Scripture

Turn to scripture for strength and encouragement during times of memory difficulty. In Isaiah 41:10, we read, *"So do not fear, for I am with you; do not be dismayed, for I am your God. I will strengthen you and help you; I will uphold you with my righteous right hand."* Let the promises of God's word bolster your faith and confidence as you navigate your memory challenges.

Practicing Patience and Perseverance

Overcoming memory challenges requires patience and perseverance. Remember that growth takes time, and setbacks are a natural part of the learning process. In James 1:4, we are reminded, *"Let perseverance finish its work so that you may be mature and complete, not lacking anything."* Keep pressing forward with faith, trusting that God is working in and through your memory struggles.

Embracing a Growth Mindset

Cultivate a growth mindset that embraces challenges and sees failures as opportunities for growth. In Philippians 4:13, we are assured, *"I can do all this through him who gives me strength."* Believe in your ability to overcome your memory challenges with God's help, and approach each obstacle with determination and resilience.

Drawing Strength from Community

Lean on the support and encouragement of your faith community as you navigate your memory challenges. In Ecclesiastes 4:9-10, we are reminded, *"Two are better than one, because they have a good return for their labor: If either of them falls down, one can help the other up. But pity anyone who falls and has no one to help them up."* Surround yourself with believers who can uplift and support you in your journey.

Celebrating Progress and Growth

Celebrate the progress and growth you experience as you overcome your memory challenges. In Psalm 118:24, we are exhorted, *"This is the day that the Lord has made; let us rejoice and be glad in it."* Rejoice in the victories, both big and small, and give thanks to God for His faithfulness in guiding you through your memory journey.

As you face your memory challenges with faith and perseverance, may you experience God's strength and provision in abundance. Remember, with God, all things are possible, including overcoming memory struggles. Amen.

CHAPTER 8

MEMORY MIRACLES IN EVERYDAY LIFE

> Explore how to apply faith-based memory techniques to everyday situations beyond scripture memorization. From academic studies to daily tasks, discover how faith can serve as a guiding light for boosting recall skills in various aspects of life.

Welcome, dear young believers. In this chapter, we explore the everyday applications of memory miracles, and the way they can enrich our lives with faith and purpose.

Remembering God's Promises

In our daily lives, we encounter moments of uncertainty, fear, and doubt. However, we can find solace and strength in remembering God's promises. In Joshua 1:9, we read, *"Have I not commanded you? Be strong and courageous. Do not be afraid; do not be discouraged, for the Lord your God will be with you wherever you go."* Let the assurance of God's presence and provisions guide you through life's challenges.

Recalling Lessons Learned

Every experience, whether joyful or challenging, offers valuable lessons for growth and maturity. By recalling and reflecting on these lessons, we gain wisdom and insight to navigate similar situations in the future. In Proverbs 4:13, we are encouraged, *"Hold on to instruction, do not let it go; guard it well, for it is your life."* Let the lessons learned from experiences inform your decisions and actions.

Retaining Knowledge and Skills

In our pursuit of knowledge and mastery, memory plays a vital role in retaining information and skills. Whether studying for exams, learning a new hobby, or honing talents, the ability to recall information and techniques is essential for success.

In Proverbs 2:10-11, we read, *"For wisdom will enter your heart, and knowledge will be pleasant to your soul. Discretion will protect you, and understanding will guard you."* Let the pursuit of wisdom and knowledge be a lifelong endeavor fueled by the miracle of memory.

Recounting Acts of Kindness and Gratitude

In a world often marked by busyness and distractions, it is easy to overlook the blessings and acts of kindness bestowed upon us. However, by intentionally recalling and recounting these moments of grace and gratitude, we cultivate a heart of thanksgiving and appreciation.

Psalm 103:2 reminds us to *"Praise the Lord, my soul, and forget not all his benefits."* Let gratitude be the melody that fills your heart and fuels your memory.

Revisiting Sacred Traditions and Rituals

Throughout history, sacred traditions and rituals have served as reminders of God's faithfulness and love. Whether observing communion, celebrating festivals, or participating in prayer and worship, these practices strengthen our faith and deepen our connection with God.

In 1 Corinthians 11:23-26, we are instructed to *"do this in remembrance of me"* during the institution of the Lord's Supper. Let the sacred traditions and rituals of your faith serve as anchors for your memory and sources of spiritual nourishment.

Reflecting on Miracles and Testimonies

The testimonies of God's faithfulness and miracles are powerful reminders of His sovereignty and love. By reflecting on these stories of divine intervention and provision, we are encouraged to trust in God's goodness and faithfulness in our own lives.

In Psalm 77:11-12, the psalmist declares, *"I will remember the deeds of the Lord; yes, I will remember your miracles of long ago.*

I will consider all your works and meditate on all your mighty deeds." Let the memories of God's miracles inspire hope and confidence in His promises.

Rejoicing in the Miracle of Salvation

Above all else, the greatest memory miracle we can experience is the gift of salvation through Jesus Christ. Ephesians 2:8-9 tells us, *"For it is by grace you have been saved, through faith— and this is not from yourselves, it is the gift of God—not by works, so that no one can boast."* Let the memory of God's redeeming grace be the foundation of your faith and the source of eternal hope.

As we go through the journey of everyday life, we hope to cherish the memory miracles that enrich our faith, inspire our hearts, and guide our paths. Let us embrace each moment as an opportunity to witness God's wonders and share His love with the world. Amen.

CHAPTER 9

THE ROLE OF COMMUNITY AND FELLOWSHIP

> Emphasize the importance of community support and fellowship in memory enhancement. Encourage children and teens to seek guidance and encouragement from their church community, fostering a supportive environment for memory growth.

In this chapter, we will explore the importance of community and fellowship in nurturing our memory skills and strengthening our faith. Communication with others a great way to enrich our capacity to remember or recall things, especially things that are common to us.

The following factors or ingredients help in achieving this aspect of our lives:

Supportive Community Bonds

God created us for fellowship and community, where we can share our joys, sorrows, and struggles with one another.

In Ecclesiastes 4:9-10 we read, *"Two are better than one, because they have a good return for their labor: If either of them falls down, one can help the other up. But pity anyone who falls and has no one to help them up."* Let us cherish the bonds of friendship and support that strengthen us on our memory journey.

Encouragement and Accountability

Within our faith communities, we find encouragement and accountability to pursue growth and excellence in our memory skills.

Hebrews 10:24-25 exhorts us, *"And let us consider how we may spur one another on toward love and good deeds, not giving up meeting together, as some are in the habit of doing, but encouraging one another—and all the more as you see the Day approaching."*

Let us uplift and inspire one another to strive for memory mastery with diligence and determination.

Shared Learning and Growth

In community settings such as youth groups, Bible studies, and Sunday schools, we have opportunities for shared learning and growth. Through group discussions, collaborative activities, and shared experiences, we deepen our understanding of God's word and its application to our lives.

In Proverbs 27:17, we are reminded, *"As iron sharpens iron, so one person sharpens another."* Let us sharpen and edify one another in our memory journey, drawing strength from our collective wisdom and insights.

Prayer and Intercession

Within our faith communities, we have the privilege of lifting one another up in prayer and intercession. Apostle James encourages us with these words, *"Therefore confess your sins to each other and pray for each other so that you may be healed. The prayer of a righteous person is powerful and effective"* (5:16). Let us intercede for one another's memory challenges, believing in the power of God to bring healing and transformation.

Celebrating Milestones and Achievements

In community, we celebrate the milestones and achievements of our fellow believers with joy and gratitude. Whether it is memorizing scripture passages, acing exams, or overcoming memory obstacles, every victory is a cause for celebration.

In Romans 12:15, we are instructed, *"Rejoice with those who rejoice; mourn with those who mourn."* Let us rejoice in the successes of our brothers and sisters, knowing that their triumphs inspire and encourage us in our own journey.

Cultivating Compassion and Empathy

Within our faith communities, we cultivate compassion and empathy for one another's struggles and challenges. In Galatians 6:2, we are reminded, *"Carry each other's burdens, and in this way you will fulfill the law of Christ."*

Let us extend grace and understanding to those who may face difficulties in their memory journey, offering our support and encouragement with love and kindness.

Embracing Diversity and Inclusion

In our diverse and inclusive faith communities, we recognize and celebrate the unique gifts and talents that each individual brings. Regardless of age, background, or ability, every member has a valuable contribution to make in our shared memory journey.

In 1 Corinthians 12:12, we are reminded, *"Just as a body, though one, has many parts, but all its many parts form one body, so it is with Christ."* Let us embrace and honor the diversity within our communities, knowing that together, we are stronger and more resilient.

As we journey together in community and fellowship, we hope that our bonds be strengthened, our faith be deepened, and our memory skills be sharpened for the glory of God. Let us walk hand in hand, supporting and encouraging one another every step of the way. Amen.

CHAPTER 10

EMBRACING GROWTH MINDSET IN MEMORY MASTERY

> Reflect on the progress made in memory development and celebrate achievements with gratitude and praise. Encourage children and teens to recognize God's blessings and faithfulness in their memory journey, inspiring continued growth and perseverance

Dear young learners, in this concluding chapter, we explore the transformative power of a growth mindset in our memory mastery journey.

As we desire growth and indeed experience it, a joy fills our hearts and reminds of the need to keep it in our minds every day.

Understanding Growth Mindset

A growth mindset is the belief that our abilities and intelligence can be developed through dedication, effort, and perseverance. It is the understanding that our talents and skills are not fixed but can grow and evolve over time with practice and learning.

Embracing Challenges

With a growth mindset, we welcome challenges as opportunities for growth and learning. Instead of being discouraged by setbacks or failures, we see them as stepping-stones to success.

In Philippians 4:13, we are assured, *"I can do all this through him who gives me strength."* Let us approach our memory challenges with confidence and determination, trusting in God's strength to guide us through.

Learning from Mistakes

Mistakes are an inevitable part of the learning process. Instead of dwelling on our errors, we embrace them as valuable lessons that propel us forward. In Proverbs 24:16, we read, *"For though the righteous fall seven times, they rise again."*

Let us rise resiliently from our mistakes, armed with newfound wisdom and insight to tackle future memory challenges.

Seeking Feedback and Guidance

In our pursuit of memory mastery, we seek feedback and guidance from mentors, teachers, and peers. Constructive feedback helps us identify areas for improvement and refine our memory techniques.

In Proverbs 19:20, we are advised, *"Listen to advice and accept discipline, and at the end you will be counted among the wise."* Let us humbly receive feedback, knowing that it fuels our growth and development.

Cultivating Perseverance and Resilience

Memory mastery requires perseverance and resilience in the face of adversity. In Romans 5:3-4, we are reminded, *"Not only so, but we also glory in our sufferings, because we know that suffering produces perseverance; perseverance, character; and character, hope."*

Let us persevere through the challenges; knowing that endurance builds character and resilience strengthens our resolve.

Celebrating Progress and Success

As we journey through our memory mastery, we celebrate our progress and successes, no matter how small they may seem.

In Psalm 118:24, we are encouraged, ***"This is the day that the Lord has made; let us rejoice and be glad in it."*** Let us rejoice in the milestones we achieve, knowing that each step forward brings us closer to our memory goals.

Inspiring Others with our Journey

Our memory mastery journey serves as an inspiration to others, motivating them to pursue their own goals with passion and determination.

In Matthew 5:16, Jesus teaches, ***"In the same way, let your light shine before others,*** *that they may see your good deeds and glorify your Father in heaven."* Let us shine brightly with the fruits of our memory efforts, inspiring those around us to embark on their own journeys of growth and discovery.

CONCLUSION

Well done going through this book. As we conclude our exploration of memory miracles and mastery, let us embrace the transformative power of a growth mindset in our lives. With faith, perseverance, and a willingness to learn, we unlock the boundless potential of our minds and hearts. We pray that our memory journeys be filled with joy, discovery, and the miraculous touch of God's grace. Amen.

Caution

Remember that while improving memory skills is valuable; do not let it overshadow the importance of rest, balance, and overall well-being. Avoid overexertion and remember to take breaks, prioritize self-care, and maintain a healthy lifestyle. Your well-being matters as much as your memory skills.

Made in the USA
Coppell, TX
29 May 2025

50066900R00056